TRUE OR FALSE

Farm Animals

BY MELVIN AND GILDA BERGER

ISBN-13: 978-0-545-00394-0
ISBN-10: 0-545-00394-6

10 9 8 7 6 5 4 3 2 1   08 09 10 11 12

Printed in the U.S.A.   23
First printing, September 2008
Book design by Nancy Sabato

All farm animals were once wild animals. **TRUE OR FALSE?**

TRUE! At one time, all animals — including horses, cows, chickens, goats, pigs, sheep, ducks, and turkeys — lived in the wild.

Then, around 12,000 years ago, people began to farm the land. They tamed a few kinds of animals to live near them. Today, farmers keep these farm animals for meat, milk, eggs, work, or as pets.

Goats and sheep were the first farm animals.

Cows usually give birth in the summer.

TRUE OR FALSE?

FALSE! Cows usually give birth in the Spring.

That's when the weather is warm and there's lots of fresh grass to eat. The newborn baby is called a calf. For five to six months, the calf drinks its mother's milk. After that, the calf grazes on grass. If the young animal is still hungry, the farmer feeds it hay or grain.

Cows (females), bulls (males), and calves (young cows and bulls) are sometimes called cattle.

A cow produces just enough milk to feed its calf.

TRUE OR FALSE?

FALSE! A cow usually produces more milk than its calf can drink.

Farmers collect the extra milk by hand or with milking machines and put it in a refrigerated storage tank. Then they send it to a factory where machines put some of the milk into bottles or cartons to sell in stores. They also use some of the milk to make butter, cheese, ice cream, or yogurt.

Brown cows give white — not chocolate — milk!

Cows chew
their food
before
swallowing. TRUE OR FALSE?

TRUE!

Cows chew their food before — and after — they swallow it!

Cows take in mouthfuls of food with their tongue and lower front teeth. They grind the food with their back teeth and swallow. Then they bring up the half-chewed food — now called cud — and chew it for six to eight hours before swallowing it again.

A cow's stomach has four separate parts; your stomach has only one!

Only female chickens lay eggs.

TRUE OR FALSE?

TRUE! Female chickens, called hens, start laying eggs when they are about five months old.

Male chickens, or roosters, never do. Some chicken eggs have white shells; some shells are brown or bluish. But all eggs are the same on the inside. Most eggs are eaten by humans.

A hen lays about 250 eggs a year!

Not all chicken eggs can hatch. **TRUE** or **FALSE?**

TRUE! Only eggs that are fertilized by a rooster can hatch into baby chickens, or chicks.

The hen lays the fertilized eggs and keeps them warm until they hatch. This can take about three weeks. On large farms, the farmer collects the eggs and sends them to a hatchery where they are kept warm until the chicks are born.

The hen rests lightly on the egg to warm, but not crush, it.

Chickens cannot fly.

TRUE
OR
FALSE?

FALSE! Chickens have wings and can fly.

But they can't go very far — only a few feet (less than 1 meter) at a time. Chickens flap their wings to fly up or down in a coop, to fight other chickens, or to escape from their enemies. Afraid that the chickens might fly away, farmers sometimes clip their feathers.

The longest chicken flight on record lasted only 13 seconds!

Roosters only crow at dawn. **TRUE** OR **FALSE?**

FALSE! Roosters crow at any time of the day or night.

Their crowing, a loud, shrill call, sends a signal to other roosters: "Stay away!" People think that roosters only crow at dawn because the morning is a quiet time and the crowing is often the first sound they hear.

Roosters often crow when an animal or person comes near.

young goats
are called kids.

TRUE
OR
FALSE?

TRUE! Young goats are called kids – just like young people are.

Bucks are adult male goats; they are also known as billy goats. Adult females are does, sometimes called nanny goats.

A nanny goat that is kidding is giving birth – not being funny!

Goats only
eat grass.

TRUE
OR
FALSE?

FALSE!

Goats also eat other plants, leaves, shoots, and twigs. They often rear up on their back legs to pull off the leaves that other animals can't reach. When there is not enough grass or leaves to go around, goats will eat the bark of trees.

Goats would sooner starve than eat food that they have stepped on or that mice have made dirty.

Most goats are unfriendly.

TRUE OR FALSE?

FALSE! Goats usually get along with all farm animals — and with people, too.

In fact, goats and horses often share stalls like good friends. Just before a horse race, people have been known to kidnap the goat from a rival horse's stall to upset that horse. This may have led to the saying, "You got my goat," which means, "You upset me."

Goats like people to scratch them — especially around their shoulders.

Only bucks have beards. TRUE OR FALSE?

FALSE! Some does have beards, too.

You can often tell a doe from a buck because the doe is usually caring for her kid. Another clue: A doe has an udder, which holds milk, between her back legs.

More people in the world drink goat milk than cow milk.

Pigs are
dirty
animals.
TRUE
OR
FALSE?

FALSE! Pigs keep themselves cleaner than most other farm animals.

But sometimes they roll around in mud to cool off. (Pigs cannot sweat.) These mud baths make people think pigs are dirty. Mud also works as a kind of sunscreen to protect their skin.

Pigs may roll in mud during the day, but the like to sleep on clean, dry straw at night.

Farmers feed mostly corn to their pigs. TRUE OR FALSE?

TRUE! A farm pig's main food is corn, with some wheat, oats, vitamins, and minerals mixed in.

But pigs will eat almost anything. They feast on roots, grass, fruit, leaves, flowers, bugs, worms, and even small animals, dead or alive.

Pigs also dine on food scraps from the kitchen or the fields and other garbage.

Female pigs give birth to one piglet at a time. **TRUE** OR **FALSE?**

FALSE!

Female pigs, called sows, usually give birth to eight to twelve piglets at a time.

The group of newborns is called a litter. The babies get milk from the sow for about three to four weeks. The piglets double their weight in the first three weeks. When fully grown, they can weigh more than 500 pounds (226.8 kilograms).

Growing young pigs usually eat 5 pounds (2.3 kilograms) of food a day!

All Sheep are white. **TRUE** OR **FALSE?**

FALSE!

There can be one or more black sheep in a group of white sheep. Most farmers prefer white sheep because their wool can be dyed other colors. Some, though, breed sheep to produce gray, silver, brown, red, or black wool for those who prefer natural colors. Today, a person may call someone who does not fit in a "black sheep."

Farmers move big herds of sheep from pasture to pasture to feed on the grass.

Farmers cut the wool from their sheep once a year.

TRUE OR FALSE?

FALSE! Sheep usually stay together in large flocks to keep safe from their many enemies.

Most sheep try to stay in the middle of the flock for the best protection. Often, a shepherd will keep the flock together and protect the sheep from wolves and other predators.

Sometimes a trained dog, donkey, or llama does the job of a shepherd.

Farm horses wear shoes.
TRUE OR FALSE?

TRUE! Farmers nail horseshoes to the bottom of their horses' feet.

(The nails don't actually hurt the horses at all.) Each foot is really a single toe. Since horses walk or run on the tips of their toes, they can easily be hurt. Horseshoes protect a horse's feet just as your shoes protect your feet.

The sole of a horse's foot never touches the ground.

Ducks lay
one egg
at a time.

TRUE
OR
FALSE?

FALSE! Female ducks lay between five and twenty-one eggs at a time!

The number of eggs depends on the breed. The eggs hatch in about a month. Two days later, the baby ducks, or ducklings, can walk, swim, and find food. But the mother duck still keeps them together and cares for them.

The ducklings' main enemies are turtles, owls, hawks, raccoons, skunks, opossums, cats, and dogs.

Farm turkeys
have red
necks.

TRUE
OR
FALSE?

TRUE!

Farm turkeys have red necks.

Some wild turkeys have necks and heads of different colors. A tom, or male turkey, also has a piece of loose, red skin that hangs from its lower jaw. This is called a wattle.

The neck of a tom turkey turns a brighter red in the spring to help it attract a mate.

Farm animals
make good
pets.

TRUE
OR
FALSE?

TRUE! Many youngsters who live in the country keep a few farm animals as pets.

Some like to care for the animals and show them at county fairs. Others simply like to play with them or watch what they do. And some enjoy training the pets and teaching them tricks.

Lambs, goats, horses, llamas, pigs, and cows are the most popular farm animal pets.

Index